The Styer-Fitzgerald
Program for Functional
Academics

Effective Strategies for Working with Paraeducators

Created by

CANDICE STYER, Ph.D.

AND

SUZANNE FITZGERALD, M.Ed.

Published by

Specially Designed
Education Services

The Styer-Fitzgerald Program for Functional Academics
Effective Strategies for Working with Paraeducators

Second Edition
First U.S. Edition Published in 2015

SPECIALLY DESIGNED EDUCATION SERVICES
18223 102ND AVE NE
SUITE B
BOTHELL, WA 98011

www.SDESworks.com

ISBN 978-0-9969130-2-7

Cover Design by

hewitt
by design

www.hewittbydesign.com

A big thank you to our editor extraordinaire, Debbie Austin.

Used by permission from The Styer-Fitzgerald Program for Functional Academics, Secondary Level
©2013 Candice Styer and Suzanne Fitzgerald, Lesson Plans and Data Sheets

Printed by CreateSpace, An Amazon.com Company

TABLE OF CONTENTS

A COPY OF THE PARAEDUCATOR HANDBOOK IS INCLUDED AT THE END OF THIS GUIDE

EFFECTIVE STRATEGIES FOR WORKING WITH PARAEDUCATORS

This teaching guide is designed to help you supervise and work with paraeducators in order to create and maintain a cohesive classroom environment.

As paraeducators are hired for your classrooms, it becomes your responsibility to provide them with training, monitor their progress, manage their schedules, address challenges, and informally evaluate their efforts. The purpose of this guide is to help you do all of these things while working together to best serve your students.*

Because each special education classroom is different—serving varied student populations with a broad spectrum of disabilities—it is important for you to tailor the information gathered from this guide to meet the specific needs of your students.

For the purposes of this manual, the terms *paraeducator*, *para*, and *assistant* are used interchangeably.

*Note: Each paraeducator needs a copy of the *Paraeducator Handbook*, available from Amazon.com, CreateSpace.com, and other retail outlets.

PART ONE: TEAM BUILDING

The information in this section is designed to assist you in creating a unified and positive work environment. These ideas can be applied to the training of new paraeducators as well as seasoned paras already working in your classroom. Experienced teachers with established personnel may find these strategies useful for improving the commitment of team members and enhancing the quality of instruction.

Chapter 1: Establishing a Positive and Professional Working Environment

This chapter offers strategies for building your team by creating rapport with your assistants and unifying your team around a classroom mission statement. Ultimately, a positive and professional environment impacts both you and your students, so it is not something to take lightly.

Getting to Know Your Paras

Many times, your paras will be used to doing things in a particular manner, and they might have more experience than you do. Having a knowledgeable paraeducator can be helpful for experienced teachers as well as for teachers just starting their careers. However, there is a fine balance between respecting their years of knowledge while maintaining your responsibility to show strong leadership. It can be intimidating, particularly for new teachers, to enter a classroom that has well-established paras. Learning how to set the standard for your classroom by providing direction can be extremely daunting. This is true regardless of years of experience in the classroom.

Consequently, the first thing that you will want to do is establish a connection with your assistants. Building a collaborative relationship with the paras already in your program will be especially helpful as you add new members to your team.

One way to do this is to set up one-on-one meetings to get to know each para on a personal and professional level. Some of the topics that you might discuss at this meeting are included below.

- What hobbies do you enjoy or what do you like to do in your free time?
- How did you become interested in becoming a paraeducator?
- How long have you been in your current position?
- How long have you been a paraeducator?
- What do you enjoy most or what is the best part of your job?
- What do you find frustrating or what is the least enjoyable part of your job?
- What has a teacher whom you have worked with done to help you do your job?
- What has a teacher whom you have worked with done that frustrates or irritates you?
- What could they have done differently?
- How have teachers demonstrated they value and respect you (for example, listen to suggestions, ask your advice or opinion)?
- How do you collaborate with the teacher and the other paras you work with directly?
- How do you collaborate with other special education teachers and paras here?
- How do you collaborate with general education teachers and staff?
- Related to collaboration, what works and what does not?
- What would you say are your strengths in the classroom?
- What are your weaknesses?

- What advice or words of wisdom would you give me as a brand new teacher starting out or as a new teacher in this program?

- Any other comments about teacher-para relationships?

Here are some additional suggestions and reminders that will assist you in building rapport with your paras.

- When you handle something differently from the way they are used to, explain to them why you are doing it differently and ask them if they have any questions or concerns.

- Be sure to show your paras that their input is valued. You can do this by encouraging them to offer suggestions about student programming. Ask them what strategies they have used in the past that have been successful. Let them be a part of the decision-making process and next steps.

- Encourage honesty and openness. Oftentimes issues arise through some kind of misunderstanding. Something that you do may unintentionally offend a team member who is used to doing things a certain way. A simple question from your para or explanation from you could make all the difference. Make sure that your paras feel comfortable asking questions.

SUZANNE'S STORY

> *When I first started teaching, I made a pretty drastic schedule change. I assumed that all of my paras would understand that the schedule would change with a new teacher entering the program. However, I didn't consider how these changes might impact my staff. I had no idea that the same para had been feeding lunch to the same student every day for the past two years. One of my schedule changes was for me to start feeding this student. It wasn't because the para was doing a poor job, but because I wanted to see if I could start teaching him to feed himself. I had just learned some new techniques for shaping a feeding program, and I was anxious to try them out.*
>
> *I made the change without taking the time to explain it to my para. Because I was new and we were just getting to know each other, she didn't feel comfortable questioning my change, and I had no idea that feeding this student was important to her. She ended up assuming that I made the change because she wasn't doing a good job. I found this out several weeks later during the student's IEP. I was explaining to his family what I was doing and why. My para was at this meeting and heard the explanation. Afterwards, she told me how relieved she was to find out that the change wasn't made because of her.*
>
> *I felt terrible that she had gone so long thinking that she had done something wrong. If I had taken the time to explain why I was making the schedule change, or if she had felt comfortable asking me why, we could've avoided the whole thing. This was the only time that we had this type of miscommunication because, going forward, I ensured that she felt comfortable questioning why I did things. I also ensured that all of my other paras felt this way.*

Developing a Classroom Mission Statement

Regardless of the size of your classroom, staff-to-student ratio, or level of student support needed, it is critical to establish how your team will function. Making sure everyone is on the "same page" encourages a cohesive, well-functioning team.

A great way to begin this process is to discuss your personal philosophy related to teaching students with disabilities. Find out how your philosophy is the same as or how it differs from other members of your team. Use this discussion as a starting point.

Next, as a team, develop a mission statement that reflects the overarching classroom philosophy and principles. Your mission statement should include some of the following components:

a. Who you are/whom you serve

b. What you believe

c. What you're going to do

d. How you're going to do it

In addition to including the above components, it is critical to ensure that all team members have input and are in agreement. Depending on the level of involvement of your administration and related service providers, such as speech and language pathologists (SLPs), occupational therapists (OTs), and physical therapists (PTs), you might want to consider involving them in the mission statement creation process as well.

Here are a few examples of classroom/school mission statements.

Sample Mission Statements

- Our mission, in partnership with parents and the community, is to provide students with the life skills and experiences that enable them to reach their fullest potential as independent thinkers. By providing a diversified curriculum and a school environment that fosters civic-mindedness, self-esteem, and respect for individual differences, we seek to address the unique needs of every student.

- Our Mission is to provide within a nurturing environment a well-balanced instructional Life Skills program that will enable all students to reach their highest level of independence. The staff is committed to creating a student-centered educational environment that stresses high expectations and addresses the physical, social, and emotional needs of students with a variety of ability levels and learning styles. Our goal is to maintain an active partnership involving students, teachers, parents, community, and staff to develop a love of learning while embracing our diversity and unique talents in a safe, challenging, respectful, and supportive environment.

- Our mission, through combined efforts of staff, parents, students, and community, is to provide students with a foundation in basic life skills, to provide an introduction to the community, to foster a positive work ethic, to create an environment that harbors tolerance and respect for each other, and to spark an attitude of inquiry and an enthusiasm for learning that will enable our children to become productive, responsible citizens.

You can find these and other sample mission statements at:

www.missionstatements.com/school_mission_statements.html.

Chapter 2: Creating Collaborative Relationships

In the field of special education, collaboration is essential. Given the nature of the environment and the number of people involved on an IEP team, you will undoubtedly work with many professionals throughout your teaching career.

The same is true for paraeducators. A basic requirement for most para positions is the ability to be a team player and work well with others. Your paraeducators should be treated as part of the team and given permission to have input regarding programs as well as receive specialized training to carry out particular therapies.

This section discusses some of the most common collaborative school relationships and provides some guidance for working together with your paras. Check with district policy regarding paraeducator involvement in parent and IEP meetings.

Collaborating with Families

As assistants in special education classrooms, your paras will have a lot of opportunities to interact not only with students but also with their families. Because paraeducators often spend more time with the student than you might be able to as the teacher, it is fitting that they would be a primary source of information in terms of reporting on the student's day. This is particularly true for paraeducators who are hired to work with students in a one-on-one capacity.

Consequently, it is important that your assistants are professional when dealing with these families. This translates primarily to being mindful of confidentiality issues. Setting up guidelines for communicating with parents is highly recommended. Be sure that if a para is going to report on behavior or other sensitive topics that they run the information by you before sending it home to families. You might also find the daily home and school checklists, provided on the Freebies page of the Styer-Fitzgerald website (www.styer-fitzgerald.com), especially useful for monitoring and maintaining communication between home and school.

It is also important to ensure that your paras understand never to discuss a student in front of other students, parents, or teachers. When specific students are discussed, it should be in a private manner or meeting format (IEP or staff meeting), the topic should be school-related, and the information kept confidential. It is essential for you and your paras to be respectful and professional when interacting with students' families. Be sure to keep communication honest and simple.

Collaborating with Administrators

Often assistants are called upon to assist administrators when they are interacting with particularly troublesome students. Or, administrators see your paras with students around the school and want to engage with them or assist in some way. Remind your paras to keep interactions professional. If an administrator asks questions or inquires about a situation, of course your para should respond appropriately, but this is not an invitation to gossip or divulge personal information about a student. Tell your paras to avoid getting caught in the middle between the family and administration. It is always best to direct others to speak to the teacher about student-specific issues and concerns. Above everything else, remind them to keep the student's best interest in the forefront always.

Collaborating with Related Service Providers

Your paraeducators will likely have frequent contact with related services personnel, such as the OT, PT, and SLP. Often, your paras will be the people implementing the speech and language or motor-related programs that these service providers have prioritized on the IEP. It is essential for your staff to have a good rapport with these providers.

Whenever possible, have your paras participate in the therapy sessions with your related service providers. A student who receives speech or physical therapy for 30 or 90 minutes per week will not be able to communicate and walk without assistance as a result of those sessions alone. For our students to reach that point, speech, communication, occupational, and physical therapy **must** be incorporated throughout the school day and week. The best way to ensure this happens is to involve your paras in student therapy sessions to receive proper training and guidance. It takes a team!

Chapter 3: Maintaining a Positive Working Environment

Once you have built rapport with your paras, written your mission statement, and created collaborative relationships, it will take some vigilance, planning, and effort on your part to maintain. In this chapter, you will find suggestions for keeping your classroom assistants happy and productive as you go forward.

Scheduling Regular Staff Meetings

To further encourage cooperation and team commitment, try to meet as a group on a regular basis. Meetings should last approximately 30 to 45 minutes and should be scheduled at a time convenient to both the teacher and the paras. During these meetings paraeducators should receive feedback about their students' programs, classroom issues, and their performance. Post an open agenda for paras to add topics as they arise between meetings. Encourage the use of initials to protect student privacy. For example, *Discuss toileting issues (DL)*. Given budget constraints and the limited time available without students present, you might need to get creative to find ways to meet as a team. Discuss with your administrator ways to schedule regular meetings throughout the year. Look at the use of "comp time" as an option.

Check in with your staff regularly to find out whether they have questions or concerns that they may not have had the time to discuss. Add these items to your staff meeting agenda if they require more in-depth coverage.

Implementing Positive Classroom Practices

Here are additional recommendations that will help you ensure that your paras benefit from a stimulating and rewarding work environment. If you take this approach, you will have loyal and hardworking assistants. These small steps of guidance and appreciation will minimize a chaotic classroom and high staff turnover.

- Being an assistant in a special education classroom is a difficult job. Consequently, it is not surprising that your paras will enjoy their jobs and feel most useful if they work in a positive environment.

- A lot can happen in a special education classroom, so it is important to deal with issues professionally and to minimize "drama." Try not to discuss issues and concerns with other members of the team.

- Be student focused! Your job is not to referee battling coworkers or take care of the adults in your classroom. You are there to make sure that you spend your day effectively teaching your students the skills they need to be as independent as possible. When issues arise, always ask yourself, "What is best for the student or my students?" When classrooms stay student-focused, issues tend to resolve themselves.

- Give your assistants permission to say they're burnt out. We are all human and will undoubtedly have moments of frustration and feelings of burnout. If you or your paras reach this point, your students and your well-being will suffer. This scenario is not good for anyone. Foster an environment that allows, without judgment, permission to ask for a change of task or person. At the same time, recognize that some students work better with certain staff and vice versa. Agree to recognize this and to not take it personally.

- Try to create a schedule that is not only consistent but also offers paras the opportunity to work with a variety of students (when appropriate). In most situations, one-to-one assistance with the same student throughout the day is not beneficial to either the student or the assistant. *However, when working with students with multiple disabilities including deaf-blindness, a one-to-one para or intervener is essential. In this circumstance, the para or intervener must have specialized training and skills in deaf-blindness and must be scheduled with that student all day.*

- Be mindful of the need to explain why you do certain things with students and why you are asking your paraeducators to perform a specific activity. For example, you can use this guidebook to explain why it is better to use the practice of hand-under-hand rather than hand-over-hand prompting, or why a special education student with dual sensory impairment needs more time to process information. As you provide explanations, your paras will be learning the reasoning behind your teaching methods. This will also help them understand why incorporating certain strategies assists rather than thwarts the progress of a student. Your clear explanations can also remove concerns your assistants might have about procedures that puzzle them or seem unhelpful (see *Suzanne's Story* on page 6).

PART TWO: EXPECTATIONS, FEEDBACK, AND EVALUATION

Chapter 4: Setting Expectations

Communicating clear expectations will help you avoid micromanaging your paraeducators. Provide strong leadership, yes, but show them that you respect their abilities and let them make decisions as issues arise. Obviously, there are some situations where you, the teacher, need to step in. However, there are many times throughout the school day your assistants, when given the opportunity, can operate with some autonomy and do just fine.

An important detail to remember when working with paraeducators is that they, like most, wish to feel productive and valued. However, in order for your assistants to feel that they are productive and doing something meaningful, they need to understand what their job duties are and how they are expected to perform them. This might seem obvious, but in the absence of guidance from the lead teacher, paras are often left on their own to determine what and how to teach their students. To avoid this, maintain an organized classroom with specific tasks assigned to each para so that each feels needed and respected professionally. Another helpful tip is to provide your assistants with "To Do" lists so they can accomplish tasks, activities, or errands during downtime or when one of their students is absent. Go to the Freebies page on the Styer-Fitzgerald website (www.styer-fitzgerald.com) for a "To Do Checklist."

Basic Expectations of Your Paraeducators

In most school districts, an administrator is responsible for evaluating your paras. Therefore, it makes sense to collaborate with your supervisor to discuss expectations for your assistants and generate a plan for ensuring that expectations are met. Some of these administrators will have limited interaction with your paras and their performances and will rely on your feedback for the evaluation process. As a team, determine requirements for your staff in order to maintain a successful program.

Even if you have been working with your team for years, it is never too late to implement expectations. Use this manual, with support from your administrator, to address some of the issues and concerns that you have been faced with over the years. What a great way to reduce stress and take some of the weight off your shoulders. Use this manual as the "bad guy."

Once your expectations are established, ask your administrator to meet with you and your team to go over them. Have your paras take notes, ask questions, and bring up any concerns about them. With your administrator's approval, tell your staff that you are required to use this manual, and then follow through. It becomes increasingly harder to enforce rules and expectations if there are no consequences. Follow through with policies from the beginning of implementation.

CANDICE'S STORY

At one time, I was managing fifteen students with severe disabilities, seven paraeducators, and two full-time nurses. When you are so overwhelmed with the many tasks and responsibilities of your day-to-day duties, it's easy to look the other way or not have the energy to address certain issues. Over time, these issues can intensify. This happened in my classroom with the use of cell phones for personal reasons and side conversations between paras. I was noticing that more of my paras' time was spent discussing their weekends than working with students. I didn't have the energy, nor did I feel like I should have to micromanage my staff, to address this issue. As it continued to get worse, I brought it up at a staff meeting. It got better for a while, but then it slipped back to the way it was. I had no plan for enforcing this rule and therefore my paras had no consequences. If I had validation, such as this manual, to implement firmer expectations in my classroom at the time, I would've jumped at the chance. I know that if I had taken the time to sit down with my supervisor to generate a plan, I would have had the full support of my administration, and we could have been a much more productive team sooner. It's never too late!

Following are some guidelines for basic expectations. Use these expectations as a starting point and perhaps a way to begin the conversation with your administration. You may modify these to meet your district's needs and, of course, add more of your own.

Attendance

Be sure your assistants understand that their attendance is vital to the day-to-day functioning of the classroom. When they are absent or frequently late, it impacts both the students and the other paraeducators. Find out what your district policy is and how it is documented and enforced. Make sure your paras understand the protocol for calling in an absence and finding coverage.

Professionalism

Encourage paraeducators to use their judgment as well as to respect their coworkers' ability to handle students and situations. Ask your paras not to intervene unless asked.

Disrespectful or negative behavior toward students and other staff should not be tolerated.

Paras should not talk about students in front of them unless they are included in the conversation. For example, in front of a student **do not** say, "Why does he make that noise?" Instead, say, "I know you are trying to tell us something, so I am going to try to find out what it is. Does anyone know what it means when _____ makes the _____noise?"

When working with students, all staff should be 100% focused. Request that they eliminate personal talk and gossip. Make it clear that the use of cell phones and other personal items should be limited to their breaks. The assistants should treat other staff and students with respect and address situations openly and directly.

Confidentiality

Make sure your paras know that no question is offensive or silly if asked appropriately. If a question is specific to a particular special education student, provide an opportunity for paras to ask you in private rather than in front of other students.

Training

Your paraeducators will be required to teach students in the special education class social, leisure, vocational, and academic skills. In addition, they will be expected to implement behavior interventions consistently and fairly as presented in a Behavior Intervention Plan. Paraeducators will require training to implement the programs with fidelity. It is your responsibility to assist them in accessing training. This could be district-wide training or ongoing, in-class training that you provide.

Data Collection

Your paraeducators will be expected to reliably collect data and record students' progress in each of their individualized programs. Training on types of data systems and strategies for gathering data should be provided by the district or by you on an ongoing, in-class basis. To get the best performance from your assistants, provide them with structured lesson plans and teaching strategies for every student that they work with. If you are using *The Styer-Fitzgerald Program for Functional Academics*, these lesson plans with corresponding data sheets are provided for you.

Expectations for Para/Student Interactions

Be sure that your assistants understand that they are important role models to the students in your special education classroom. A paraeducator's job involves many different and equally important duties. In addition to providing academic support, paras are also responsible for monitoring and working with students on appropriate behavior and social skills. There are several ways that paras can foster healthy relationships with and for their students.

Explain to your paraeducators that you set high standards and expectations for your special education students. Let them know that

- having a disability does not give a special education student an excuse for poor behavior;
- you expect staff to behave positively and in an age-appropriate manner with your special education students;
- all staff are expected to monitor students at all times including breaks to ensure on-task and appropriate behavior. When a student takes a break, it's not meant to be a break for staff.

Paraeducators are expected to encourage appropriate interactions and intervene when a student's behavior is inappropriate or harmful. Following are some standards to help guide interactions with students.

- Your paraeducators can practice greetings and simple communication and social skills with your special education students. Ask your paras to follow through while greeting to be sure that the student gives the appropriate response. The same is true when asking simple questions. It is very common to casually say "good morning" to a student without waiting or listening for a response. Teach your paras to become aware of how they are addressing students and to take the time to ensure that they respond appropriately. These skills will serve the students well in the future both socially and vocationally.

- Many special education students do not pick up on the intricacies of social skills from watching their peers. Your assistants can facilitate teaching these important skills by modeling appropriate behaviors and also by reinforcing these behaviors as they occur throughout the day.

- Your paraeducators can also create opportunities for your special education students to converse with typically developing peers by showing them how to relate with their peers using symbols and augmentative communication devices. Have paras help facilitate conversations but caution them to do it with the students, not for them.

Chapter 5: Providing Feedback and Evaluation

Give your assistants clear, constructive, and ongoing feedback. Just as everyone likes to know what their job responsibilities are, they also like to know how they are doing. Consequently, it is important to provide feedback to your assistants when they are doing a good job, as well as when they may need to make changes. Considering effective teaching/management strategies, you want to give 10 positive affirmations for each corrective suggestion when commenting on a para's performance.

Provide recognition of the accomplishments of your assistants. Let them know that you appreciate their contribution to your classroom and especially to the growth of your special education students. There are many ways to recognize your paraeducators. For example, write a personal thank-you note or give a small token of appreciation such as a coffee card with a certificate of appreciation (like the example on the next page). Make a comment while the para is working with a student about the quality of the para's (verbal) reinforcements. The point is to be proactive and acknowledge the hard work they do with your students.

The following are a few examples of statements of appreciation and acknowledgement:

- "We appreciate your incredible dedication to our students."
- "I admire your positive teaching style!"
- "Your instructional strategies and data collection skills are excellent."
- "I appreciate the way you connect with our kids personally."
- "You inspire everyone with how you advocate for our kids and educate others about disabilities."

Frequently, your para's formal evaluation process is conducted by one of the school administrators. Sometimes these same administrators don't have the opportunity to observe your paraeducators to the degree needed to do a valid evaluation of their skills. If this is the case, try having your administrator drop in at scheduled times to observe a paraeducator working on a particular program with a specific student. If this is not possible, request that you have input into the administrator's report. A professional evaluation should be a tool for goal setting and problem solving and, therefore, must reflect the para's skills accurately.

A modifiable, printable version of this certificate can be found on the Freebies page of the Styer-Fitzgerald website, www.styer-fitzgerald.com.

PART THREE: TRAINING

Another key factor in creating a cohesive and effective classroom environment is to make sure that your paraeducators are well-trained in specific areas. The training that you provide or help set up for your assistants should include the following topics. These topics are covered in more detail in the following chapters.

- Disability awareness, including how to manage at risk and/or disruptive behaviors
- Effective strategies for instructional delivery
- Data collection

Chapter 6: Teaching Disability Awareness and Etiquette

It is important to educate your paras about general disability awareness and etiquette, to help them learn how to handle difficult situations that may arise, and to teach them to work with students who are non-verbal or difficult to understand.

As we settle into routines and go about our daily tasks, it is easy to forget basic protocol, particularly when working with students who use wheelchairs or who have vision and/or hearing impairments. It is extremely difficult to get beyond the hearing and sighted perspective. Following are some basic reminders about communication and etiquette.

Have your paraeducators read the section titled "Disability Awareness" in the *Paraeducator Handbook* and then lead them through Activities #1 and #2.

Communication

Discuss with your paraeducators the many ways that special education students communicate with others. Explain how communication can happen through one or more of these ways:

- Verbal
- Tactile
- Sign language
- Modified sign language
- Assistive technology (iPads, devices, switches, computers)
- Facial expressions
- Gestures
- Utterances
- Eye gaze
- Modified "yes" or "no"
- Pictures and picture symbols

Communicating with Non-Verbal Students

If a paraeducator does not understand a special education student, he or she should not pretend to do so. Instead have the para follow these steps:

1. Ask the student to repeat the communication.
2. Say, "I really want to know what you are saying. Please be patient with me and tell me again."
3. If you still do not understand, say, "I still don't understand what you just told me, so I'm going to find another staff person to help me understand."
4. Say, "Thank you for being so patient with me. I really wanted to know what you said."

Remind your paraeducators that:

- Just because someone cannot speak does not mean he or she does not understand.
- It is important to include non-verbal students in conversations about their communication. For example, if you are talking to the SLP about changes to a student's communication system, you will say to the student, "Joe, I am going to talk to Ms. Smith about the new words that we are adding to your iPad." It shows that you care and that you want to understand what they are saying.

The special education student who is non-verbal might not be able to respond to the paraeducator in a conventional manner. Remember, communication goes beyond basic wants and needs. It's important for students to also be able to make comments and have conversations. Following are some suggestions for your paras to try with students that they are having difficulty maintaining a conversation or communicating with.

- Ask other staff for items or activities the student enjoys.
- Ask the student if there are any pictures she can share with you that tell you about her.
- Brainstorm as a team ideas about other topics to discuss with individual students.
- Refer to websites and search video topics for other tips and ideas. For example, your paraeducators can refer to the Washington Sensory Disabilities Services (WSDS—in Washington State) website at www.wsdsonline.org.
- If available, obtain a list of suggested conversation topics and age-appropriate step-by-step social scripts.

Resource Note: Ideas are available, for example, on the "Can We Chat" CD by Linda J. Burkhart and Caroline Ramsey Musselwhite. This CD is available at *www.lindaburkhart.com*. These are sources you as a teacher would use but likely not provide in the paraeducator information.

Activity #1—Communicating Appropriately

Activity #1

It is important that your paraeducators understand the different ways in which your special education students communicate. Discuss the different types and methods of communication with your assistants, using examples of the students in your classroom.

Tips for Working with Students in Wheelchairs

If you have special education students who are in wheelchairs, review the following etiquette tips with your paraeducators.

- To move a person or take a student who is in a wheelchair to another location, remember to give a warning before moving him or her. Many special education students have heightened startle reflexes and might be easily upset without first knowing what to expect. Following are a few suggestions for letting the student know what you will be doing.

  1. Tap the student on the shoulder and move to a place where he or she can see and hear you.

2. Begin with the student's name and say, "_____, we are going to go to _____ now, and I'm going to push you there."

3. Say, "Are you ready?" or "Here we go."

- If a student is not in his or her wheelchair and you need to move the chair, let the student know what you intend to do and where you will be moving their chair.

- **Never** hold onto or sit in a student's empty wheelchair—the wheelchair is part of the student's personal space so doing so is tantamount to sitting on their lap.

Tips for Working with Hearing-Impaired, Visually-Impaired, or Deaf-Blind Students

- For students who are deaf, blind, or deaf-blind, instead of speaking, use whatever method of communication is appropriate for that student (sign language, tactile symbols, touch cues, etc.).

- If you have a student who is deaf and has an interpreter, be sure to talk to the student and not to the interpreter.

- If you have a student who is blind, talk about what is going on around him or her. For example, "Did you hear the door close? Sally Smith just came into the classroom; she's hanging up her coat."

- As you approach someone who has a dual sensory impairment (deaf-blindness), begin by tapping the person on the shoulder. Then move your hand down the arm until you reach his or her hand; then give your identifier. An identifier is a familiar object that the student has learned to associate with specific people. For example, your identifier might be a ring because your student identifies you by the ring that they always touch when they feel for your hand.

  Remember that some students with deaf-blindness often have some hearing and vision. If that is the case, identify yourself verbally or show them your picture so they know who you are.

- When working with students who are deaf-blind, be sure to put your hands underneath their hands rather than grabbing the tops of their hands and manipulating them. This is called "hand-under-hand" and it is less intrusive than grabbing a student by the hand. In addition to being less intrusive, hand-under-hand also allows the student more control and encourages them to move toward independence with much more ease and efficiency.

- When you walk with a student who is blind or deaf-blind, offer your arm. Watch for and warn about changes in the terrain, transition strips, doorways, etc. At all times you must be aware of your surroundings so that you can guide the student safely.

Students with multiple disabilities, including deaf-blindness, require special training methods and accommodations to succeed as learners. If you serve these students, we encourage you to seek further training and resources. For more information, contact Specially Designed Education Services (SDES) at www.sdesworks.com.

Other resources:

- National Center on Deaf-Blindness www.nationaldb.org
- Find out if your state has a Deaf-Blind Project. Washington State's Deaf-Blind Project is www.wsdsonline.org.

Handling Inappropriate Behaviors

This section will cover suggestions on how to handle students that act inappropriately in some social situations. Strategies for dealing with students that display more disruptive and violent behavior are not addressed in this manual. There are many good guidebooks that provide information relevant to handling students that present more severe behavioral issues. In addition, these types of students typically require an observation and planning for a robust intervention, which is beyond the scope of this manual.

The following example will be helpful to your assistants if they encounter a situation where a student is trying to get their attention in an inappropriate way. Explain to your paraeducators that your special education students might inadvertently invade personal space when they are trying to get attention. It is common for our special education students, who are typically unaware or unsure about how to communicate their feelings, to act improperly. For example, a student who wants your attention might give your para a hug and not let go or grab the para's hand or arm without asking permission instead of simply talking to the para. Explain to your assistants that if a student enters their personal space, there are ways to respond, depending on the severity of the situation. Offer your paras the following suggestions for things to say in such situations.

- "You are in my personal space and you need to back up."

- "This is my space. That is your space. Do not enter my space."

- "You are making me uncomfortable and you need to stop."

- "That is inappropriate. Stop, please."

- For elementary school paraeducators specifically, tell them that they can say, "You didn't ask if you could hug me. You need to ask." Even if a special education student asks first, let your paras know that they are not obligated to say "yes" and sometimes, it is good to say "no."

- With an older student, suggest that your assistants say something like, "I'm your teacher, and you are my student. It's not appropriate for us to hug. You hug people in your family." As students mature, setting appropriate physical boundaries becomes essential. As our students get older and begin spending more time in the community, the issue of safety becomes a reality. As difficult as it may be to refrain from physical reinforcement (i.e., hugs), it is critical to provide these boundaries in order for students to be successful and safe in the community.

Activity #2—Helpful Responses

Following is an example of when a para might be unsure about how to respond to a special education student. Let your paraeducators know this is not unusual but that it is important to learn an appropriate response for future situations. Before acting or responding, your assistants should ask themselves, *"How will my response help this student in the future?"*

Activity #2

Have your paraeducators read the following scenario. Provide them with other real-life situations that reflect your students' individual challenges.

Jane is a sophomore with cerebral palsy and intellectual disabilities. She becomes very excited around her friends and loves to talk. She has a difficult time initiating conversation and regulating the volume of her voice. She has just asked you a question and you answered it, yet she continues asking the same question at least five more times, getting louder and louder each time.

Here are two possible ways to respond to Jane:

- Answer her question again a couple of times then ignore her for a few times.
- Answer her the first time only. When she asks again, tell her, "I've already answered you, Jane. I'm not going to answer again."

Explain to your paras that the first response might seem like the nice thing to do, but it will not help Jane in the future. If you keep answering her and then ignoring her, she will continue to repeat the same behavior, always asking her questions over and over. Jane is a very sociable person, but no one will want to be around her if she is continuously asking the same question in a loud voice.

Explain that the second response might appear harsh. But if you do not engage with her, Jane will learn that she needs to ask only once before moving on to another question or topic. The second response will help teach her. How does this response help Jane in the future? Because she is a very sociable person, Jane MUST learn to be socially appropriate. If she learns these skills, the people around her will become more accepting of her, she will have friends, and she can experience a more fulfilling life. If she does not learn these skills, people will avoid her, and as she gets older, she could become more isolated from the very society she craves.

Again, stress that sometimes the difficult reactions are those that will help students the most. Tell your paras that if they are unsure about how to respond to a situation, they should ask you for guidance or add it to the staff meeting agenda so you can brainstorm as a team. The more consistent you are, the better!

Chapter 7: Teaching Instructional Strategies

In this section we will introduce some basic methods that have been shown to be successful when working with students with disabilities. Helping your paraeducators to understand the methodology of working with special education students is essential to their success in the classroom. This section will prepare you to teach your assistants how to use prompts, reinforcement, and correction procedures as well as to track an individual student's progress.

The following sections on prompting, reinforcement, and correction procedures are also presented in the *Paraeducator Handbook.* Present the information in this section, using the activities (3, 4, 5, and 6) to demonstrate and then practice the concepts.

If you are using *The Styer-Fitzgerald Program for Functional Academics* curriculum in your classroom, more detailed information about these teaching strategies can be found in the Teaching Guide and on the Styer-Fitzgerald Training Session Videos found on the Styer-Fitzgerald website (www.styer-fitzgerald.com).

Teaching Paraeducators to Use Prompts

An important component of a powerful instructional environment involves using prompts or cues in a cohesive and effective manner. In addition, the type of prompt or cue that tells students what it is you are asking them to do will differ depending on the skill being taught. For example, in a community setting, the prompt or cue can be the sign at the crosswalk that flashes "Don't Walk." On the other hand, in the classroom during a teaching session, the prompt or cue is the teacher (or para) giving an instruction—for example, "Give me $4.99," or "What time is it?"

It is important for your paras to understand not only how to use prompts in different environments but also to know how to determine when the level of prompting should be faded with fewer or no prompts being provided during instruction. Your paraeducators can refer to the "Using Prompts" section in their handbooks for review.

Use Activity #6, Prompting, Reinforcement, and Correction Procedures Practice (page 38), to practice using these instructional strategies. Be sure to emphasize the following points.

Prompts during Direct Instruction

Again, the type of prompts or cues that your paras will need to use will vary depending on the skills they are teaching. Following are pointers when teaching a skill in the classroom (direct instruction).

- Make the prompts clear. Tell special education students exactly what you want them to do. For example, "Give me $4.99."

- Vary the prompts so that students learn that a variety of cues have the same meaning (for example, you can say, "$4.99" or "That will be $4.99.").

Money Management, Bills B—Next-Dollar Strategy (Phase I)

Long Term Goal:	Short Term Objective:
Student will use money in the community to purchase items of up to $5.00.	Student will count from $0.01 to $5.00 using ones.

Materials: Ten one-dollar bills

Notes:

Be sure to stop the student as soon as he or she makes a mistake. Then model the correct response and have him/her try again.

Ask students randomly for less than $1 amounts (.57, .25, etc.) along with even amounts (e.g., $1.00, $2.00, etc.).

If a student is verbal, have him/her count out loud—this is helpful in determining when mistakes are made.

Prompt	Correct Response	Correction Procedure	Data
Enter the price into the calculator and say, "Give me _____ (e.g., *$2.99*)."	Student counts out three one-dollar bills for _____ (e.g., *$2.99*).	Say, "Stop. Watch me." Model the correct response. Repeat the prompt. If needed, say, "Count with me." Count with the student. Next, say, "Your turn." Have the student count again on his/her own. Reinforce the correct response. For amounts under a dollar, say, "Stop. When all you hear is *cents*, you give me a dollar." Repeat the prompt (e.g., *Ninety-nine cents*).	**Correct Response:** Circle the corresponding number on the data sheet. **Incorrect Response:** Put a slash through the corresponding number on the data sheet.

Prompts in the Real Environment

When teaching a skill in the community (real environment), your paras will be using the prompts or cues that occur naturally in that environment. For example, at a street corner, rather than using a verbal prompt of "Stop," you will want your assistants to point to the "Walk/Don't Walk" sign and say, "That sign says *Walk*; that means go." Or say, "That sign says *Don't Walk*; that means stop or wait." This technique allows students to respond to the stimuli in the situation (e.g., the green light) rather than to the instructor's verbal cue, "Go/ Walk." See example lesson plan under Fading Prompts for community-based activity.

Fading Prompts

When paraeducators are teaching a skill initially, their prompts should be frequent and concise. After the student begins to learn a skill in the real environment, the para should give him/her the chance to respond on his/her own before providing additional prompts. As a student learns a skill, the need for prompting decreases, thus, the para can start to "fade" the cues. Fading the cue in the real world, at the right time, is essential to the student being able to use the skill independently. Even when students are becoming fluent with a skill, they may still have difficulty on some of the steps of the activity. When this situation occurs, students may require some prompting but at a reduced level.

For example, using the example above, the teacher would say to the student, "That sign says *Walk*, so what do you need to do?" In this way you, the teacher, or your assistant are still pointing out the relevant cue (i.e., "The sign says *Walk*"), but you are not telling the student exactly how to respond to the cue.

Encourage your paras to practice fading prompts in everything they do throughout the school day. For example, when the bell rings, instead of telling your students to check their schedules, wait and see how they respond.

If a prompt is needed, instead of saying, "There's the bell. Check your schedule," fade your prompt to "There's the bell. What do you need to do?" In an elementary classroom, when it's time for recess, instead of telling your students, "It's cold outside. Get your coat," wait and see how they respond. If a prompt is needed, say, "It's time for recess, and it's cold outside. What do you need?"

Community-Based Training—Street Crossing

Long Term Goal:	Short Term Objective:
Student will cross streets safely within the community.	Student will cross controlled and uncontrolled streets/ intersections safely.

Materials: N/A

Notes:

Make a reusable Task Analysis by copying and laminating the reduced size Task Analysis found in the *Reproducible Teaching Materials* binder. Add a hook for a belt or lanyard for easy transport. Use a dry-erase marker to record data and erase after transferring data to final task analysis sheet.

Correction procedures:

- Tell the student to "stop" or "wait," interrupting the behavior chain; this is better than having to go back and correct the behavior later.
- Repeat the S^D. Use the S^D/cue that matches the student's level of skill acquisition (Initial Acquisition or Fading). See "Prompting" section in the *Curriculum* Teaching Guide.

Correction Procedure

S^D Prompt		Correct Response	Initial Acquisition of Skills *when student is first learning*	Fading Prompts *after student has begun learning*	Data
Uncontrolled	At curb	Stops	"Stop/Wait." "You are at the curb (S^D). You need to wait." OR "The light is red (S^D).You need to wait."	"Stop/Wait." "You are at the curb (S^D). What do you do?" OR "The light is red (S^D). What do you do?"	Record the number of prompts per step.
	Waiting	Looks both ways			
	Clear	Crosses the street			
Controlled	At curb	Stops	"Now that you're waiting (S^D), you need to look in both directions." OR "Now that you're waiting (S^D), you need to look for the light to turn green." "The street is clear (S^D), it is safe to cross now." OR "The light is green (S^D), you need to cross now."	"Now that you're waiting (S^D), what are you looking for?" "The street is clear (S^D). What do you do now?" OR "The light is green (S^D). What do you do now?"	
	Waiting	Looks at light			
	Green light	Crosses the street			
	Red light	Continues to wait			

Teaching Reinforcement and Correction Procedures

As you train your paras, introduce reinforcement and correction procedures simultaneously. Presenting these concepts together is important because both procedures are necessary in order for special education students to learn new skills. Students learn new skills or behaviors when their responses are immediately met with reinforcement (usually verbal) for correct responses or a correction procedure for an incorrect response. Because reinforcement and correction procedures are equally important teaching tools, it is essential that your paraeducators understand how to use them.

The following diagram illustrates the relationship between prompts, reinforcement, and correction procedures.

Prompt ➡ Correct Response ➡ Reinforcement

Prompt ➡ Incorrect Response ➡ Correction Procedure

Reinforcement

By reinforcing a correct response or behavior, you increase the likelihood of the reoccurrence of that behavior. In other words:

BEHAVIOR > SOMETHING "GOOD" HAPPENS > BEHAVIOR IS LIKELY TO REOCCUR
(*Reinforcement*)

TYPES OF REINFORCEMENT

It is important that your paraeducators understand that there are different types of reinforcement. They also need to know which method is most impacting and to know when and how to use each type effectively. The following information will be helpful in guiding your paras when determining the type of reinforcement to use with particular students. Discuss the three types of reinforcement—verbal, physical, and tangible—that your paras will be using when they are teaching their students.

Verbal Reinforcement

Verbal reinforcement consists of praise or other words of encouragement. For example, "I like how you are staying on task." Or, "You really are working hard!"

Physical Reinforcement

There are different levels of physical reinforcement, and each needs to be age appropriate. For example, a hug might be appropriate for an elementary-aged student, whereas a pat on the back or a "high five" is more fitting when working with a secondary-aged student.

Tangible Reinforcement

These are items that a student can touch that have reinforcing properties. Examples of tangible reinforcement can include items such as a paycheck, a token, a card with break choices, or a certificate of work well-done.

DETERMINING THE TYPE OF REINFORCEMENT TO USE

Your paraeducators should understand that the needs of an individual student or the particular lesson being taught often determines the type of reinforcement that will be appropriate. The type of reinforcement is also often a matter of preference of a specific special education student, and what works with one student may or may not be effective with another.

Your assistants can combine different types of reinforcement. For example, saying, "Nice work" while giving a "high five" combines verbal with physical reinforcement. In addition, your paras can take advantage of activities like break times and build them into your instructional session using them as reinforcement.

FREQUENCY OF REINFORCEMENT

The frequency, or how often reinforcement occurs, depends on where the student is in his or her learning process. Paraeducators need to understand when to use continuous versus intermittent reinforcement.

Continuous Reinforcement Schedule

Deliver this method of reinforcement after each and every correct response. Continuous reinforcement is generally used when a student is initially learning a skill.

Intermittent Reinforcement Schedule

Deliver this method of reinforcement after a random number of correct responses. Intermittent reinforcement is generally used when a student has learned a skill but still requires periodic feedback about his or her performance. When you are fading from responding to every behavior to randomly responding, you are using an intermittent reinforcement strategy.

DELIVERING REINFORCEMENT

It is important that your paraeducators understand the essential concepts of delivering reinforcement. It is vital to their students' learning process that reinforcement be delivered following these guidelines:

- Reinforcement needs to be delivered immediately following the behavior. That way the student is clear about what he/she did to elicit the reinforcement.

- Reinforcement needs to be direct and clearly state what the student did that resulted in the reinforcement. For example, telling a student "good job" doesn't actually tell the student what "job" caused them to be reinforced. Instead, if the student is told, "You are doing a good job of sitting quietly," then he/she knows that it is the quiet sitting behavior that produced the reinforcement.

- When first teaching a skill, the reinforcement should be delivered frequently (i.e., on a continuous schedule). Again, it is important to be aware of when it is suitable to reduce or fade the reinforcement and go to an intermittent schedule. If fading does not happen in a timely way, your student is likely to become satiated with the reinforcement. If this occurs, the reinforcement will no longer hold value and will be ineffective in increasing or maintaining the desired behavior or skill.

Activities #3 and #4—Reinforcement

Activity #3

Have paraeducators brainstorm about reinforcement examples that they have found successful. If they are familiar with your special education students, ask them to name some of the reinforcers to which specific students respond.

Activity #4

Ask paraeducators to think of different ways to say "good job" (refer paraeducators to Appendix A in the *Paraeducator Handbook*).

Note: Another helpful strategy is to post examples of verbal reinforcement in your classroom so that all staff can review these samples as needed.

Correction Procedures

Using correction procedures appropriately will facilitate learning and increase the skill levels of special education students as effectively as positive reinforcement does. It is important that your paraeducators understand how to use correction procedures effectively so that special education students will learn from their mistakes.

Remind your assistants to use correction procedures in a way that will be educational rather than injurious to a student's self-esteem. Following are some tips on how to phrase a response to an incorrect answer.

Be positive. Avoid saying, "No, that's not right." This type of response is not educational because it does not tell the student what he/she did incorrectly. This response does not take advantage of the teachable moment. To do so, the instructor should say, "The answer is …," or "The clock says …," or "This is $3.99."

After you have corrected the student by showing him/her the correct response, give him/her a chance to try again.

The following steps illustrate an effective correction procedure:

1. When there is a mistake, say, "Stop" or "Wait" so that the mistake does not continue and become ingrained as part of the skill.

2. Then say, "Watch me." (Model the behavior, such as: "This is $1.20," and count out the amount.)

3. Then say, "Now you try."

4. Then reinforce the correct response. Say, "That's right. That is $1.20."

Activity #5—Correction Procedures

Activity #5

Have paraeducators role-play a one-to-one teaching session and practice both reinforcing correct responses and using correction procedures for incorrect responses.

Begin by having a para play the role of one of the special education students in your class with you in the role as teacher, modeling both reinforcement and correction procedures.

After demonstrating the teacher-student interaction, have your paraeducators practice in the role of the teacher.

Find a Lesson Plan to use for this activity in Appendix B in the *Paraeducator Handbook*.

Summary of Reinforcement and Correction Procedures with Lesson Samples

Remind your paraeducators

- When they use reinforcement and correction procedures, they need to be delivered immediately and clearly.

- The response or behavior that previously occurred will be strengthened if it is followed up immediately with verbal praise (reinforcement). This also keeps the student engaged and motivated to work hard.

- Clear and **specific** praise helps a student understand exactly what he or she did correctly. For instance, saying, "Nice job" lets the student know that he did the right thing, but it does not tell the student what the right thing was. It is better to be specific and say, for example, "Nice job counting out $4.99."

- It might be difficult for your paraeducators to correct special education students because they do not want to hurt their feelings. But assure them that when they use correction procedures appropriately, the students are learning. The experience becomes educational rather than ego-deflating.

REINFORCEMENT SAMPLE

The following sample is taken from lessons presented in *The Styer-Fitzgerald Program for Functional Academics* Curriculum. Note the reinforcement for the correct response.

Using reinforcement to teach a skill:

Prompt	Correct Response	Reinforcement
Say, "Give me $4.99."	Student counts out five one-dollar bills.	Say, "Nice job giving me $4.99."

CORRECTION PROCEDURE SAMPLE

The following sample is taken from lessons presented in *The Styer-Fitzgerald Program for Functional Academics* Curriculum. Note the correction procedure for the incorrect response.

Prompt	Response	Correction Procedure
Say, "Give me $4.99."	Student counts, "One, two, four."	When the student makes the mistake, immediately say, "Stop." Repeat the prompt: "$4.99." Say, "Watch me; one, two, three, four, ninety-nine. Now it's your turn."

The example shows how the teacher stops the student immediately when the mistake is made or, in this case, when the number three is skipped. Therefore, the student does not learn that four follows two in the sequence. If you do not stop the student at the point of the mistake and he or she keeps counting, the sequence learned is "one, two, four..." rather than "one, two, three, four..."

After stopping the student, you must clearly demonstrate the correct response. In other words, say, "Watch me. This is $4.99" as you count out "one, two, three, four..."

It is natural to want to just say "no," give the student the correct answer, and then move on to the next question. However, doing this does not provide the student with the information needed to learn the skill you are trying to teach.

Activity #6—Prompting, Reinforcement, and Correction Procedures Practice

> ### *Activity #6*
>
> Have your paraeducators role-play teaching a skill such as telling time by quarter hours as in this sample from *The Styer-Fitzgerald Program for Functional Academics* Curriculum.
>
> | Prompt | Correct Response | Correction Procedure | Data |
> |---|---|---|---|
> | **Verbal students:** Present the student with the clock and ask, "What time is it?"

Non-verbal students: Use three cards rather than an analog clock. Say, "Show me ____ (e.g., *9:30*)." | **Verbal students:** Student says the correct time (e.g., *9:30*).

Non-verbal students: Student points to the correct card. | Say, "No. It is _____ (e.g., *9:30*)."

Repeat the prompt (with the same time, e.g., *9:30*) and ask "What time is it?" (verbal)

Or "Show me ____." (non-verbal)

Reinforce the correct response. | **Correct Response:** Circle the corresponding number on the data sheet.

Incorrect Response: Put a slash through the corresponding number. |
>
> Begin by having your paras play the role of the special education student as you model prompting, reinforcement, and correction procedures. Next, change roles and have them practice their teaching skills.
>
> Find a Lesson Plan to use for this activity in Appendix B of the *Paraeducator Handbook*.

Chapter 8: Teaching Data Collection

Data is initially used to evaluate a student's present level of performance and to determine where each student's baseline is in different skill areas. Collect additional data to track student progress and to determine when to move on to the next level of the skill sequence.

Data is also used to analyze whether to make changes to individual student programs. For example, if a student has made little or no progress, the data is helpful in determining to stop teaching a skill or to break the skill into easier segments.

This paraeducator guide references the two primary types of data collection as described in *The Styer-Fitzgerald Program for Functional Academics*. If you are using the Functional Academics program in your classroom, it is recommended that you review the "Data Recording" section in the Curriculum. The two most used methods of data collection are

- Discrete Trial format
- Task Analysis format

Discrete Trial—Recording the Percentage Correct

In a discrete trial data system, your paraeducators will be recording correct responses with circles and incorrect responses with slashes. This will allow you, the teacher, to summarize the data by calculating the overall percentage correct over the total number of instructional trials for each skill area.

Following is an example of a discrete trial data sheet with sample data.

The discrete trial data sheet is the type your paras will be using when teaching skills such as time telling or counting money.

Date:	9/1	9/2	9/3											Correct
	10	10	10	10	10	10	10	10	10	10	10	10	10	100%
	9	9	9	9	9	9	9	9	9	9	9	9	9	90%
	8	8	8	8	8	8	8	8	8	8	8	8	8	80%
	7	7	7	7	7	7	7	7	7	7	7	7	7	70%
	6	6	6	6	6	6	6	6	6	6	6	6	6	60%
	5	5	5	5	5	5	5	5	5	5	5	5	5	50%
	4	4	4	4	4	4	4	4	4	4	4	4	4	40%
	3	3	3	3	3	3	3	3	3	3	3	3	3	30%
	2	2	2	2	2	2	2	2	2	2	2	2	2	20%
	1	1	1	1	1	1	1	1	1	1	1	1	1	10%

Prompt: "Give me _____."

Example: Discrete Trial Data Sheet

Task Analysis—Recording the Number of Prompts

The task analysis format is generally used to count the number of prompts per step that are required for a student to perform a particular task or skill. Teach your paraeducators to record the number of prompts per session until the student can perform the entire task independently.

If a student has difficulty with a particular step, you, the teacher, will need to break the task into smaller/simpler steps until the student can perform the task independently.

The task analysis format is the type of data sheet your paras will use when they teach skills in the community, such as street crossing and grocery shopping. Here is an example of a task analysis sheet with sample data.

	Task Analysis	Initials: *AB* Date: *9/1* Prompts	Initials: *AB* Date: *9/4* Prompts	Initials: Date: Prompts	Initials: Date: Prompts	Initials: Date: Prompts
1	Finds nearest bus stop	//	/			
2	Finds bus number	/	/			
3	Gets on correct bus	//	//			
4	Pays/shows pass	/	/			
5	Finds a seat	//	/			
6	Pulls cord prior to stop	/	/			
7	Exits the bus	/	/			
	Total Number of Prompts	10	8			
	Bus Stop Location	3rd & Main	B Street			
	Final Destination	17th St.	J Street			

Example: Task Analysis Data Sheet—Number of Prompts

Task Analysis—Recording the Type of Prompts

You will also encounter a Task Analysis data collection system that tracks the type of prompts if you are working with the elementary level of *The Styer-Fitzgerald Program for Functional Academics* Curriculum.

For example, when teaching a self-help skill to students, you may be monitoring whether the prompts were verbal, gesture, or physical. The decision to use one type of prompt over the other one will be made on a case-by-case basis and depend on the learning style of each individual student.

Student: _Bev_   **Year:** _2014_

Note: This data sheet is designed to track the type of prompt. Use the following key to determine which prompt was used per step. Circle the corresponding letter.

P = Physical   **G** = Gesture   **V** = Verbal   **I** = Independent

Task Analysis	Initials: SF	Initials: CS	Initials:	Initials:	Initials:
	Date: 4/1	Date: 4/2	Date:	Date:	Date:
	Prompts	Prompts	Prompts	Prompts	Prompts
1 Turns on hot/cold water	P G (V) I	P G (V) I	P G V I	P G V I	P G V I
2 Picks up soap	P (G) V I	P G (V) I	P G V I	P G V I	P G V I
3 Rubs soap on hands	P (G) V I	P G (V) I	P G V I	P G V I	P G V I
4 Rinses off soap	P G (V) I	P G V (I)	P G V I	P G V I	P G V I
5 Turns off water	P (G) V I	P G (V) I	P G V I	P G V I	P G V I
6 Dries hands	(P) G V I	(P) G V I	P G V I	P G V I	P G V I
Total Number of Physical Prompts	1	1			
Total Number of Gestural Prompts	3	0			
Total Number of Verbal Prompts	2	4			
Total Number of Independents	0	1			

Example: Task Analysis Data Sheet—Type of Prompts

Accuracy in Data Collection

It is not uncommon for paraeducators to misunderstand what constitutes a prompt and to mark data sheets incorrectly. Be sure to monitor your assistants when they are tracking a student's progress. Training and practice will help them accurately use the two primary systems of collecting data. It is important that your paras understand that they are not being mean when they are marking a student's response incorrect. The rule for recording a response as correct or incorrect is as follows: If the para reinforces the student's initial response, the response is marked as correct. However, if the para is required to do a correction procedure, the response should be marked as incorrect even if the student goes on to respond accurately after having been shown the correct answer.

Instruct your paraeducators to initial the days that they collect data. This will be helpful if you need to investigate and account for unusual data on a particular date. It is also a good idea to have your paras note on the data sheets any dates that a student's performance might have been affected by illness, lack of sleep, or classroom interruptions.

Activity #7—Practice Gathering Data

Activity #7

Have paraeducators role-play a couple of lessons using both types of data sheets. Have one para take data while you and another assistant role-play instruction. Be sure all of the paraeducators have a chance to collect both types of data. Check their work and make constructive comments to ensure their accuracy.

Find Data Sheets to use for this activity in Appendix C of the *Paraeducator Handbook*.

Before paraeducators begin working with your special education students, have them observe you, or other seasoned paras, as you work with students. After new assistants are comfortable with the programs they have observed, have them teach the skill to the students. Do not require new paras to record data until they are comfortable with prompting, reinforcement, and correction procedures. Then, periodically observe them to be sure their data collection skills are reliable.

Part Three: Training

We hope that this manual has been helpful in providing a comprehensive guide to hiring and managing your support staff. The training and support that you are able to provide to your paras will have a significant impact on the cohesiveness and efficiency of your classroom. A positive work environment benefits everyone—you, your paras, and most important of all, your students.

Notes

Notes

Notes

About the Authors

Together, Dr. Candice Styer and Suzanne Fitzgerald have over 40 years of classroom experience both as paraeducators and as teachers working with paraeducators. They were inspired to write this manual based on their own experiences and the experiences of other teachers and paras with whom they have consulted.

Dr. Candice Styer has worked in the field of special education for over 30 years. She received her teaching certification, M.Ed., and Ph.D. at the University of Oregon. She developed the life skills assessment and curriculum over the last 30 years while teaching middle school and high school students with moderate and severe disabilities.

Suzanne Fitzgerald has worked with children and adults with developmental, physical, emotional, and behavioral disabilities in classroom, vocational, residential, and recreational settings for the past 21 years. She received her Bachelor of Arts degree in Human Services from Western Washington University and her teaching certification and Masters in Special Education degree from the University of Washington. Suzanne was a middle and high school special education teacher for the Snohomish School District.

Additional Curriculum by Dr. Candice Styer and Suzanne Fitzgerald

The Styer-Fitzgerald Program for Functional Academics

A unique approach to teaching functional skills to students with mild, moderate, and severe disabilities, including autism. The comprehensive assessment and curriculum teach independent skills that focus on each student's individual needs. Teachers themselves, Candice and Suzanne developed and tested the program in classrooms serving students with a variety of disabilities.

Elementary Level

- 11 Academic and Life Skills Units
- Teaching Guide with Implementation Tools
- Program Masters (includes Lesson Plans and Data Sheets)
- Portfolio Teacher's Manual
- Over 200 pages in reproducibles, including Teaching Materials, Progress-Tracking Data Sheets, Curriculum Progress Guide, Present Levels of Performance Chart, Student Portfolio Forms
- Assessment Teacher's Manual
- Assessment Testing Kit
- Teaching Materials Kit (included in Deluxe Teaching Package)

Secondary Level

- 10 Academic and Life Skills Units
- Teaching Guide with Implementation Tools
- Program Masters (includes Lesson Plans and Data Sheets)
- Portfolio Teacher's Manual
- Over 100 pages of reproducibles, including Teaching Materials, Progress-Tracking Data Sheets, Curriculum Progress Guide, Present Levels of Performance Chart, Student Portfolio Forms
- Assessment Teacher's Manual
- Assessment Testing Kit
- Teaching Materials Kit (included in Deluxe Teaching Package)

Additional Titles:

Life after School: Transition Planning for Students with Disabilities

Titles Available on Amazon.com, CreateSpace.com, and other retail outlets:

**Effective Strategies for Working with Paraeducators
Paraeducator Handbook**

**Teacher's Guide to Peer Tutoring
Peer Tutor Handbook**

For more information, please visit the Styer-Fitzgerald website at www.SDESworks.com.

The Styer-Fitzgerald Program for Functional Academics

Paraeducator Handbook
(Teacher's Copy)

Created by

CANDICE STYER, Ph.D.

AND

SUZANNE FITZGERALD, M.Ed.

Published by

Specially Designed
Education Services

The Styer-Fitzgerald Program for Functional Academics
Paraeducator Handbook

Second Edition
First U.S. Edition Published in 2015

SPECIALLY DESIGNED EDUCATION SERVICES
18223 102ND AVE NE
SUITE B
BOTHELL, WA 98011

www.SDESworks.com

ISBN 978-0-9969130-3-4

Cover Design by

hewitt
by design

www.hewittbydesign.com

A big thank you to our editor extraordinaire, Debbie Austin.

Used by permission from The Styer-Fitzgerald Program for Functional Academics, Secondary Level
©2013 Candice Styer and Suzanne Fitzgerald, Lesson Plans and Data Sheets

Printed by CreateSpace, An Amazon.com Company

Contents

Introduction to the Paraeducator Handbook

This guide is designed to provide you with information about your job requirements and the expectations of you, as a team player, in our special education classroom.

Classroom Mission Statement

_____

_____

_____

_____

_____

_____

_____

_____

_____

Job Expectations

Attendance

Your attendance is vital to the day-to-day functioning of the classroom. When you are absent or late, it impacts both the students and your coworkers. When you need to be away from your job, please try to plan ahead so that appropriate coverage can be arranged.

Professionalism

It is important to have a positive attitude and to act in an age-appropriate manner with students in the special education classroom. Disrespectful or negative behavior is not tolerated. Respect your coworkers' abilities to handle students and situations, and only intervene when asked. When you are working with students be 100% focused. Eliminate personal talk and gossip, and limit the use of cell phones and other personal items to your break times. Treat other staff and students with respect and address situations openly and directly.

Confidentiality

No question is offensive or silly if asked appropriately. If a question is specific to a particular special education student, ask the teacher in private rather than in front of other students or coworkers.

Training

You will be required to assist with teaching students social, leisure, vocational, and academic skills. In addition, you are expected to implement behavior interventions consistently and follow the steps outlined in specific interventions. This manual will help you learn instructional strategies to use in the classroom with the students. You will receive additional training throughout the year.

Data Collection

You will be expected to reliably collect data and record students' progress in each of their individualized programs.

Student Interaction

You are an important role model to the students in your special education classroom. Your job involves many different and equally important duties. In addition to providing academic support, you are also responsible for monitoring and working with students on appropriate behavior and social skills.

We have set high standards and expectations for our special education students. Keep in mind that

- Having a disability does not give a special education student an excuse for poor behavior.
- You are expected to behave positively and in an age-appropriate manner with your special education students.
- You are expected to monitor students at all times (including during their breaks) to ensure on-task and appropriate behavior.

You are also expected to encourage appropriate interactions and intervene when a student's behavior is inappropriate or harmful. Following are some standards to help guide interactions with students.

- You can practice greetings and simple communication and social skills with your special education students. When you greet a student, be sure that the student gives the appropriate response. The same is true when asking simple questions. It is very common to casually say "good morning" to a student without waiting or listening for a response. Be aware of how you are addressing students and take the time to ensure that they respond appropriately. These skills will serve the students well in the future both socially and vocationally.
- Many special education students do not pick up on the intricacies of social skills from watching their peers. You can facilitate teaching these important skills by modeling appropriate behaviors and also by reinforcing these behaviors as they occur throughout the day.
- You can also create opportunities for your special education students to converse with typically developing peers by showing them how to relate with their peers using symbols and augmentative communication devices. Help facilitate these conversations but do it with the students, not for them.

Additional Expectations

Disability Awareness

It is important to be educated about general disability awareness and etiquette and to learn how to handle difficult situations that may arise. It is also helpful to learn how to work with students who are non-verbal or difficult to understand. The information in this section will be useful in increasing your knowledge about teaching students with more challenging issues or multiple disabilities.

Communication

Remember that there are many ways that special education students communicate with others. Communication can happen through one or more of these ways:

- Verbal
- Tactile
- Sign language
- Modified sign language
- Assistive technology (iPads, devices, switches, computers)
- Facial expressions
- Gestures
- Utterances
- Eye gaze
- Modified "yes" or "no"
- Pictures and picture symbols

Steps for Communicating with Non-verbal Students

If you do not understand a special education student, you should not pretend to do so. In such an instance, you can follow these steps:

1. Ask the student to repeat the communication.
2. Say, "I really want to know what you are saying. Please be patient with me and tell me again."
3. If you still do not understand, say, "I still don't understand what you just told me, so I'm going to find another staff person to help me understand."
4. Say, "Thank you for being so patient with me. I really wanted to know what you said."

Here are some things to remember when working with your students:

- Just because someone cannot speak does not mean he or she does not understand.
- Do not talk about students in front of them unless they are included in the conversation. For example, in front of a student **do not** say, "Why does he make that noise?" Instead, say, "I know you are trying to tell us something, so I am going to try to find out what it is. Does anyone know what it means when _____ makes the _____ noise?"

- It is important to include non-verbal students in conversations about their communication. It shows that you care and that you want to understand what they are saying.

Carrying on a conversation with someone who is non-verbal can be difficult. The special education student might not be able to respond to you in a conventional manner. Following are some suggestions for you to try with students that you may be having difficulty communicating with.

- Ask other staff about items or activities a particular student enjoys.
- Ask the student if there are any pictures she can share with you that tell you about her.
- Brainstorm as a team ideas about other topics to discuss with individual students.
- Refer to websites and search video topics for other tips and ideas. For example, you can refer to the Washington Sensory Disabilities Services website (WSDS—in Washington State) at www.wsdsonline.org.
- If available, obtain a list of suggested conversation topics and age-appropriate step-by-step social scripts.

Tips for Working with Students in Wheelchairs

If you have special education students who are in wheelchairs or who have vision or hearing impairments, you will want to review the following etiquette tips.

- To move a person or take a student who is in a wheelchair to another location, give a warning before moving him or her. Many special education students have heightened startle reflexes and might be easily upset without first knowing what to expect. Following is one strategy for letting the student know what you will be doing.
  1. Tap the student on the shoulder and move to a place where he or she can see and hear you.
  2. Begin with the student's name and say, "_____, we are going to go to _____ now, and I'm going to push you there."
  3. Say, "Are you ready?" or "Here we go."
- If a student is not in his or her wheelchair and you need to move the chair, let the student know what you intend to do and where you will move it.
- **Never** hold onto or sit in a student's empty wheelchair—the wheelchair is part of the student's personal space.

Tips for Working with Hearing-Impaired, Visually-Impaired, or Deaf-Blind Students

- If you have a student who is deaf and has an interpreter, be sure to talk to the student and not to the interpreter.
- If you have a student who is blind, talk about what is going on around him or her. For example, "Did you hear the door close? Sally Smith just came into the classroom; she's hanging up her coat."
- As you approach someone who has a dual sensory impairment (deaf-blindness), begin by tapping the person on the shoulder. Then move your hand down the arm until you reach his or her hand; then give

your identifier. An identifier is a familiar object that the student has learned to associate with specific people. For example, your identifier might be a ring because your student identifies you by the ring that they always touch when they feel for your hand. (Go to www.pathstoliteracy.org/blog/using-personal-identifiers-my-deafblind-son/ for more information.) Remember that some students with deaf-blindness often have some hearing and vision. If that is the case, identify yourself verbally or show them your picture so they know who you are.

- When working with students who are deaf-blind, be sure to put your hands underneath their hands rather than grabbing the tops of their hands and manipulating them. This is called "hand-under-hand," and it is less intrusive than grabbing a student by the hand.

- When you walk with a student who is blind or deaf-blind, offer him/her your arm. Watch for and warn them about changes in the terrain, transition strips, doorways, etc. At all times you must be aware of your surroundings so that you can guide them safely.

Handling Inappropriate Behaviors

This section will cover suggestions on how to handle students that act inappropriately in some social situations.

The following example will be helpful if you encounter a situation where a student is trying to get your attention in an inappropriate way. It is important to understand that sometimes our special education students inadvertently invade personal space when they are trying to get attention. It is common for our special education students, who are typically unaware or unsure about how to communicate their feelings, to act inappropriately. For example, a student who wants your attention might give you a hug and not let go or grab your hand or arm without asking permission instead of simply talking to you. If a student enters your personal space, there are ways to respond, depending on the severity of the situation. Following are some suggestions for things to say in such situations.

- "You are in my personal space and you need to back up."

- "This is my space. That is your space. Do not enter my space."

- "You are making me uncomfortable and you need to stop."

- "That is inappropriate. Stop, please."

- If you work in an elementary classroom, you can say, "You didn't ask if you could hug me. You need to ask." Even if a special education student asks first, you need to know that you are not obligated to say "yes" and sometimes, it is good to say "no."

- With an older student you can say something like, "I'm your teacher; you are my student. It's not appropriate for us to hug. You hug people in your family." As students mature, setting appropriate physical boundaries becomes essential. As our students get older and begin spending more time in the community, the issue of safety becomes a reality. As difficult as it may be to refrain from physical reinforcement (i.e., hugs), it is critical to provide these boundaries in order for students to be successful and safe in the community.

Notes

Using Prompts

An important component to providing a cohesive instructional environment is to use prompts or cues in an efficient and effective manner. In addition, the type of prompt or cue that tells students what it is you are asking them to do will differ depending on the skill being taught. For example, in a community setting, the prompt or cue can be the sign at the crosswalk that flashes "Don't Walk." On the other hand, in the classroom during a teaching session, the prompt or cue is the teacher (or you) giving an instruction—for example, "Give me $4.99," or "What time is it?"

It is important to understand not only how to use prompts in different environments but also to know how to determine when the level of prompting should be faded with fewer or no prompts being provided during instruction.

Prompts during Direct Instruction

As stated previously, the type of prompts or cues that you will need to learn to use will vary depending on the skills you are teaching. Following are some pointers when teaching a skill in the classroom (direct instruction).

- Make the prompts clear. Tell special education students exactly what you want them to do. For example, "Give me $4.99."

- Vary the prompts so that students learn that a variety of cues have the same meaning (for example, you can say "$4.99" or "That will be $4.99.")

Next-Dollar Strategy

Long-Term Goal:	Short-Term Objective:
Student will use money in the community to purchase items up to $5.00.	Student will count from $0.01 to $5.00 using ones.

Materials: Ten One-Dollar Bills

Notes:

Be sure to stop the student as soon as he or she makes a mistake. Then model the correct response and have him/her try again.

Ask students randomly for less than $1 amounts (.57, .25, etc.) along with even amounts (e.g., $1.00, $2.00, etc.).

If a student is verbal, have him/her count out loud—this is helpful in determining when mistakes are made.

Teach this program in conjunction with Calculator Skills.

Prompt	Correct Response	Correction Procedure	Data
Enter the price into the calculator and say, "Give me _____ (e.g., $2.99)."	Student counts out three one-dollar bills for $2.99.	Say, "Stop. Watch me." Model the correct response. Repeat the prompt. If needed, say, "Count with me." Count with the student. Next, say, "Your turn." Have the student count again on his/her own. Reinforce the correct response. For amounts under a dollar say, "Stop. When all you hear is *cents*, you give me a dollar." Repeat the prompt—e.g., "Ninety-nine cents."	**Correct Response:** Praise and circle the corresponding number on the data sheet. **Incorrect Response:** Put a slash through the corresponding number on the data sheet.

Prompts in the Real Environment

When teaching a skill in the community (real environment), you will be using the prompts or cues that occur naturally in that environment. For example, at a street corner, rather than using a verbal prompt of "Stop," you will want to point to the "Walk/Don't Walk" sign and say, "That sign says *Walk*; that means go." Or say, "That sign says *Don't Walk*; that means stop or wait." This technique allows students to respond to the stimuli in the situation (e.g., the green light) rather than to your verbal cue, "Go/Walk." See example lesson plan under Fading Prompts for community-based activity.

Fading Prompts

When you are teaching a skill initially, your prompts should be frequent and concise. After the student begins to learn a skill in the real environment, you need to give him/her the chance to respond on his/her own before providing additional prompts. As students learn a skill, the need for prompting decreases, thus, you can start to "fade" the cues. Fading the cue in the real world, at the right time, is essential to the student being able to use the skill independently. Even when students are becoming fluent with a skill they may still have difficulty on some of the steps of the activity. When this situation occurs, students may require some prompting but at a reduced level. For example, using the example above, you would say to the student, "That sign says *Walk*, so what do you do?" In this way you are still pointing out the relevant cue (i.e., "The sign says *Walk*"), but you are not telling the student exactly how to respond to the cue.

Community-Based Training—Street Crossing

Long Term Goal:	Short Term Objective:
Student will cross streets safely within the community.	Student will cross controlled and uncontrolled streets/intersections safely.

Materials: N/A

Notes:

Make a reusable Task Analysis by copying and laminating the reduced size Task Analysis found in the *Reproducible Teaching Materials* binder. Add a hook for a belt or lanyard for easy transport. Use a dry-erase marker to record data and erase after transferring data to final task analysis sheet.

Correction procedures:

- Tell the student to "stop" or "wait," interrupting the behavior chain; this is better than having to go back and correct the behavior later.
- Repeat the S^D. Use the S^D/cue that matches the student's level of skill acquisition (Initial Acquisition or Fading). See "Prompting" section in the *Curriculum* Teaching Guide.

Correction Procedure

	S^D Prompt	Correct Response	Initial Acquisition of Skills when student is first learning	Fading Prompts after student has begun learning	Data
Uncontrolled	At curb	Stops	"Stop/Wait." "You are at the curb (S^D). You need to wait." OR "The light is red (S^D).You need to wait."	"Stop/Wait." "You are at the curb (S^D). What do you do?" OR "The light is red (S^D). What do you do?"	Record the number of prompts per step.
	Waiting	Looks both ways			
	Clear	Crosses the street			
Controlled	At curb	Stops	"Now that you're waiting (S^D), you need to look in both directions." OR "Now that you're waiting (S^D), you need to look for the light to turn green." "The street is clear (S^D), it is safe to cross now." OR "The light is green (S^D), you need to cross now."	"Now that you're waiting (S^D), what are you looking for?" "The street is clear (S^D). What do you do now?" OR "The light is green (S^D). What do you do now?"	
	Waiting	Looks at light			
	Green light	Crosses the street			
	Red light	Continues to wait			

Notes

Reinforcement

By reinforcing a correct response or behavior you increase the likelihood of the reoccurrence of that behavior. In other words:

BEHAVIOR > SOMETHING "GOOD" HAPPENS > BEHAVIOR IS LIKELY TO REOCCUR
(*Reinforcement*)

Types of Reinforcement

There are different types of reinforcement. It is important to know which method is best to use as well as when and how to use each type effectively. The following information will be helpful when determining the type of reinforcement to use with particular students.

Verbal Reinforcement

Verbal reinforcement consists of praise or other words of encouragement. For example, "I like how you are staying on task." Or, "You really are working hard!"

Physical Reinforcement

There are different levels of physical reinforcement, and each needs to be age appropriate. For example, a hug might be appropriate for an elementary-aged student whereas a pat on the back or a "high five" is more fitting when working with a secondary-aged student.

Tangible Reinforcement

These are items that a student can touch that have reinforcing properties. Examples of tangible reinforcement can include items such as a paycheck, a token, a card with break choices, or a certificate of work well done.

Determining the Type of Reinforcement to Use

The needs of an individual student or the particular lesson being taught often determines the type of reinforcement that will be appropriate. The type of reinforcement is also often a matter of preference of a specific special education student so what works with one student may or may not be effective with another.

You can combine different types of reinforcement. For example, saying "Nice work," while giving a "high five" combines verbal with physical reinforcement. In addition, you can take advantage of activities like break times and build them into your instructional session using them as reinforcement.

Frequency of Reinforcement

The frequency of how often reinforcement occurs depends on where the student is in his or her learning process.

Continuous Reinforcement Schedule

Deliver this method of reinforcement after each and every correct response. Continuous reinforcement is generally used when a student is initially learning a skill.

Intermittent Reinforcement Schedule

Deliver this method of reinforcement after a random number of correct responses. Intermittent reinforcement is generally used when a student has learned a skill but still requires periodic feedback about his or her performance. When you are fading from responding to every behavior to randomly responding, you are using an intermittent reinforcement strategy.

Delivering Reinforcement

Understanding the essential concepts of how to deliver reinforcement is as important as the type of reinforcement you are using. It is vital to the student's learning process that reinforcement be delivered following these guidelines:

- Reinforcement needs to be delivered immediately following the behavior. That way the student is clear about what he/she did to elicit the reinforcement.

- Reinforcement needs to be direct. Clearly state what the student did that resulted in the reinforcement. For example, telling a student "good job" doesn't actually tell the student what "job" caused them to be reinforced. Instead, if the student is told, "You are doing a good job of sitting quietly," then he/she knows that it is the quiet sitting behavior that produced the reinforcement.

- At least when first teaching a skill, the reinforcement should be delivered frequently (i.e., on a continuous schedule). Again, it is important to be aware of when it is suitable to reduce or fade the reinforcement and go to an intermittent schedule. If fading does not happen in a timely way, your student is likely to become satiated with the reinforcement. If this occurs, the reinforcement will no longer hold value and will be ineffective in increasing or maintaining the desired behavior or skill.

Notes

Correction Procedures

Using correction procedures appropriately will facilitate learning and increase the skill levels of your students as effectively as positive reinforcement does. It is important that you understand how to use correction procedures effectively so that your students will learn from their mistakes.

Be sure that you use correction procedures in a way that is educational rather than injurious to a student's self-esteem. Following are some tips on how to phrase a response to an incorrect answer.

Be positive. Avoid saying, "No, that's not right." This type of response is not educational because it does not tell the student what he/she did incorrectly. This response does not take advantage of the teachable moment. To do so, you should say, "The answer is …," or "The clock says …," or "This is 3.99."

Once you've corrected the student by showing him/her the correct response, give him/her a chance to try again.

The following steps illustrate an effective correction procedure:

1. When there is a mistake, say, "Stop" or "Wait," so that the mistake does not continue and become ingrained as part of the skill.
2. Then say, "Watch me." (Model the behavior, such as: "This is $1.20," and count out the amount.)
3. Then say, "Now you try."
4. Then reinforce the correct response. Say, "That's right. That is $1.20."

Lesson Samples of Reinforcement and Correction Procedures

The following diagram illustrates the relationship between prompts, reinforcement, and correction procedures.

Prompt ➡ **Correct Response** ➡ **Reinforcement**

Prompt ➡ **Incorrect Response** ➡ **Correction Procedure**

Here are some reminders about how to use reinforcement and correction procedures to teach a skill.

- The response or behavior that previously occurred will be strengthened if it is followed up immediately with verbal praise (reinforcement).

- Clear and **specific** praise helps a student understand exactly what he or she did correctly. For instance, saying "nice job" lets the student know that he did the right thing, but it does not tell the student what the right thing was. It is better to be specific and say, for example, "Nice job counting out $4.99."

- Be assured that when you use correction procedures appropriately you will not be hurting the student's feelings. Instead, you will be helping them learn.

Reinforcement Sample

The following sample is taken from lessons presented in *The Styer-Fitzgerald Program for Functional Academics* Curriculum. Note the reinforcement for the correct response.

Using reinforcement to teach a skill:

Prompt	Correct Response	Reinforcement
Say, "Give me $4.99."	Student counts out five one-dollar bills.	Say, "Nice job giving me $4.99."

Correction Procedure Sample

The following sample is taken from lessons presented in *The Styer-Fitzgerald Program for Functional Academics* Curriculum. Note the correction procedure for the incorrect response.

Prompt	Response	Correction Procedure
Say, "Give me $4.99."	Student counts, "One, two, four."	When the student makes the mistake, immediately say, "Stop." Repeat the prompt: "$4.99." Say, "Watch me; one, two, three, four, ninety-nine. Now it's your turn."

The example shows how to stop the student immediately when the mistake is made or when the number three is skipped. Therefore, the student does not learn that four follows two in the sequence. If you do not stop the student at the point of the mistake and he or she keeps counting, the sequence learned is "one, two, four..." rather than "one, two, three, four..."

After stopping the student, you must clearly demonstrate the correct response. In other words, "Watch me. This is $4.99" as you count out "one, two, three, four..."

It is natural to want to just say "no," give the student the correct answer, and then move on to the next question. However, doing this does not provide the student with the information needed to learn the skill you are trying to teach.

Notes

Data Collection

Data is initially used to evaluate a student's present level of performance and to determine where each student's baseline is in different skill areas. Additional data is collected to track a student's progress and to determine when to move on to the next level of the skill sequence.

Data is also used to analyze whether to make changes to an individual student's programs. For example, if a student has made little or no progress, data would be helpful in determining to stop teaching a skill or to break the skill into easier segments.

The two primary types of data collection described in *The Styer-Fitzgerald Program for Functional Academics* are Discrete Trial and Task Analysis data systems.

The following sections define these format types and show a sample of each type of data sheet.

Discrete Trial—Recording the Percentage Correct

In a discrete trial data system, you will be recording correct responses with circles and incorrect responses with slashes. This will allow you to summarize the data by calculating the overall percentage correct over the total number of trials of instruction for each skill area.

Following is an example of a discrete trial data sheet with sample data. The discrete trial data sheet is the type you will be using when teaching skills such as time-telling or counting coins.

Date:	9/1	9/2	9/3											Correct
	10	10	10	10	10	10	10	10	10	10	10	10	10	100%
	9	9	9	9	9	9	9	9	9	9	9	9	9	90%
	8	8	8	8	8	8	8	8	8	8	8	8	8	80%
	7	7	7	7	7	7	7	7	7	7	7	7	7	70%
	6	6	6	6	6	6	6	6	6	6	6	6	6	60%
	5	5	5	5	5	5	5	5	5	5	5	5	5	50%
	4	4	4	4	4	4	4	4	4	4	4	4	4	40%
	3	3	3	3	3	3	3	3	3	3	3	3	3	30%
	2	2	2	2	2	2	2	2	2	2	2	2	2	20%
	1	1	1	1	1	1	1	1	1	1	1	1	1	10%

Prompt: "Give me _____."

Task Analysis—Recording the Number of Prompts

The task analysis format is generally used to count the number of prompts per step that are required for a student to perform a particular task or skill. If a student has difficulty with a particular step, you will need to break the task into smaller/simpler steps until the student can perform the task independently.

The task analysis format is the type of data sheet you will use when teaching skills in the community, such as street crossing and grocery shopping. Here is an example of a task analysis sheet with sample data.

Task Analysis		Initials: AB	Initials: AB	Initials:	Initials:	Initials:
		Date: 9/1	Date: 9/4	Date:	Date:	Date:
		Prompts	Prompts	Prompts	Prompts	Prompts
1	Finds nearest bus stop	//	/			
2	Finds bus number	/	/			
3	Gets on correct bus	//	//			
4	Pays/shows pass	/	/			
5	Finds a seat	//	/			
6	Pulls cord prior to stop	/	/			
7	Exits the bus	/	/			
Total Number of Prompts		10	8			
Bus Stop Location		3rd & Main	B Street			
Final Destination		17th St.	J Street			

Task Analysis—Recording the Type of Prompt

You will encounter this type of data collection system if you are working with the elementary version of *The Styer-Fitzgerald Program for Functional Academics* Curriculum. For example, when teaching a self-help skill to students, you may need to track the type of prompts that you are providing, as opposed to the number of prompts. The decision to use one type of prompt over the other one will be made on a case-by-case basis and depend on the learning style of each individual student.

Student: __*Bev*__   Year: __*2014*__

Note: This data sheet is designed to track the type of prompt. Use the following key to determine which prompt was used per step. Circle the corresponding letter.

P = Physical   **G** = Gesture   **V** = Verbal   **I** = Independent

	Task Analysis	Initials: *SF*	Initials: *CS*	Initials:	Initials:	Initials:
		Date: 4/1	Date: 4/2	Date:	Date:	Date:
		Prompts	Prompts	Prompts	Prompts	Prompts
1	Turns on hot/cold water	P G (V) I	P G (V) I	P G V I	P G V I	P G V I
2	Picks up soap	P (G) V I	P G (V) I	P G V I	P G V I	P G V I
3	Rubs soap on hands	P (G) V I	P G (V) I	P G V I	P G V I	P G V I
4	Rinses off soap	P G (V) I	P G V (I)	P G V I	P G V I	P G V I
5	Turns off water	P (G) V I	P G (V) I	P G V I	P G V I	P G V I
6	Dries hands	(P) G V I	(P) G V I	P G V I	P G V I	P G V I
	Total Number of Physical Prompts	1	1			
	Total Number of Gestural Prompts	3	0			
	Total Number of Verbal Prompts	2	4			
	Total Number of Independents	0	1			

Accuracy in Data Collection

It is not uncommon to misunderstand what constitutes a prompt and to mark data sheets incorrectly. Training and practice will help you accurately use the two primary systems of collecting data. It is important that you understand that you are not being mean when you are marking a student's response incorrect. The rule for recording a response as correct or incorrect is as follows: If you reinforced the student's initial response, the response is marked as correct. However, if you had to do a correction procedure, the response should be marked as incorrect even if the student went on to respond accurately after having been shown the correct answer.

It is helpful if you put your initials on the days that you collect data. It is also a good idea to note on the data sheets any dates that a special education student's performance might have been affected by illness, lack of sleep, or classroom interruptions.

Now that you have completed your training, you are better prepared to face the challenges of the classroom in which you will work. You have chosen a profession that is both rewarding and arduous. Know that the skills that you possess as a teacher will have a life-long impact on your students. What you do with them every day will change their lives as well as your own.

Notes

Appendix A

Pointers for Giving Praise

When you praise one of your special education students, be specific and encourage the response or behavior you want to see again. Here are some suggestions:

"Nice job...

paying attention."

following directions."

listening to instructions."

acting like an adult."

speaking like an adult."

staying on task."

working hard."

"I like how you...

are in your own space."

are sitting like an adult."

have your hands and feet to yourself."

are following directions."

are listening to directions."

are trying hard."

are acting like a high school student."

are *now* using a quieter tone of voice."

Some Other Words of Praise

"You're doing a much better job working."

"That's the way to act like an adult."

"Thank you for working quietly."

"I'm so glad you made the right choice."

Appendix B

Use the lesson plans for the activities led by the teacher during training.

Activity #5 Lesson Plan: Next-Dollar Strategy

Long-Term Goal:	Short-Term Objective:
Student will use money in the community to purchase items up to $5.00.	Student will count from $0.01 to $5.00 using ones.

Materials: Ten One-Dollar Bills

Notes:

Be sure to stop the student as soon as he or she makes a mistake. Then model the correct response and have him/her try again.

Ask students randomly for less than $1 amounts (.57, .25, etc.) along with even amounts (e.g., $1.00, $2.00, etc.).

If a student is verbal, have him/her count out loud—this is helpful in determining when mistakes are made.

Teach this program in conjunction with Calculator Skills.

Prompt	Correct Response	Correction Procedure	Data
Enter the price into the calculator and say, "Give me _____ (e.g., $2.99)."	Student counts out three one-dollar bills for $2.99.	Say, "Stop. Watch me." Model the correct response. Repeat the prompt. If needed, say, "Count with me." Count with the student. Next, say, "Your turn." Have the student count again on his/her own. Reinforce the correct response. For amounts under a dollar say, "Stop. When all you hear is *cents*, you give me a dollar." Repeat the prompt—e.g., "Ninety-nine cents."	**Correct Response:** Praise and circle the corresponding number on the data sheet. **Incorrect Response:** Put a slash through the corresponding number on the data sheet.

Activity #6 Lesson Plan: Telling Analog Time by Quarter Hours

Long-Term Goal:	Short-Term Objective:
Student will tell time on an analog clock.	Student will tell time by 15-minute, 30-minute, 45-minute, and one-hour increments.

Materials: Analog clock; Three cards with times (only for non-verbal students)

Notes:

For students who have difficulty with telling time by 15, 30, and 45 minutes, break the skill into two sections. First, teach time by the hour and half-hour (Level B1); then add 15 and 45 (Level B2).

Prompt	Correct Response	Correction Procedure	Data
Verbal students: Present the student with the clock and ask, "What time is it?" **Non-verbal students:** Use three cards rather than an analog clock. Say, "Show me _____ (e.g., 9:30)."	**Verbal students:** Student says the correct time. **Non-verbal students:** Student points to the correct time (e.g., 9:30).	Say, "No. It is _____ (e.g., 9:30)." Repeat the prompt (with the same time, 9:30) and ask "What time is it?" (verbal) or "Show me _____." (non-verbal) Reinforce the correct response.	**Correct Response:** Praise and circle the corresponding number on the data sheet. **Incorrect Response:** Put a slash through the corresponding number.

Appendix C

Use the data sheets for the activities led by the teacher during training.

Activity #7 Data Sheet: Next-Dollar Strategy

Student: _____   **Year:** _____

Circle the correct responses and mark a line through incorrect responses. To see a graph of the student's progress, in each column, draw a square around the number that represents the percentage correct; then connect the squares with a line. The "1" through "10" represents both the number of trials on a given day and the percentage correct.

Prompt: "Give me _____."   **$0.01 – $5.00**

Date:												Correct
10	10	10	10	10	10	10	10	10	10	10	10	100%
9	9	9	9	9	9	9	9	9	9	9	9	90%
8	8	8	8	8	8	8	8	8	8	8	8	80%
7	7	7	7	7	7	7	7	7	7	7	7	70%
6	6	6	6	6	6	6	6	6	6	6	6	60%
5	5	5	5	5	5	5	5	5	5	5	5	50%
4	4	4	4	4	4	4	4	4	4	4	4	40%
3	3	3	3	3	3	3	3	3	3	3	3	30%
2	2	2	2	2	2	2	2	2	2	2	2	20%
1	1	1	1	1	1	1	1	1	1	1	1	10%

Prompt: "Give me _____."   **$0.01 – $5.00**

Date:												Correct
10	10	10	10	10	10	10	10	10	10	10	10	100%
9	9	9	9	9	9	9	9	9	9	9	9	90%
8	8	8	8	8	8	8	8	8	8	8	8	80%
7	7	7	7	7	7	7	7	7	7	7	7	70%
6	6	6	6	6	6	6	6	6	6	6	6	60%
5	5	5	5	5	5	5	5	5	5	5	5	50%
4	4	4	4	4	4	4	4	4	4	4	4	40%
3	3	3	3	3	3	3	3	3	3	3	3	30%
2	2	2	2	2	2	2	2	2	2	2	2	20%
1	1	1	1	1	1	1	1	1	1	1	1	10%

Activity #7 Data Sheet: Telling Analog Time by Quarter Hours

Student: _____   **Year:** _____

Circle the correct responses and mark a line through incorrect responses. To see a graph of the student's progress, in each column, draw a square around the number that represents the percentage correct; then connect the squares with a line. The "1" through "10" represents both the number of trials on a given day and the percentage correct.

Prompt: "What time is it?" or "Show me _____."

Response: Student either says or points to the correct time.

Date:													Correct
10	10	10	10	10	10	10	10	10	10	10	10		100%
9	9	9	9	9	9	9	9	9	9	9	9		90%
8	8	8	8	8	8	8	8	8	8	8	8		80%
7	7	7	7	7	7	7	7	7	7	7	7		70%
6	6	6	6	6	6	6	6	6	6	6	6		60%
5	5	5	5	5	5	5	5	5	5	5	5		50%
4	4	4	4	4	4	4	4	4	4	4	4		40%
3	3	3	3	3	3	3	3	3	3	3	3		30%
2	2	2	2	2	2	2	2	2	2	2	2		20%
1	1	1	1	1	1	1	1	1	1	1	1		10%

Prompt: "What time is it?" or "Show me _____."

Response: Student either says or points to the correct time.

Date:													Correct
10	10	10	10	10	10	10	10	10	10	10	10		100%
9	9	9	9	9	9	9	9	9	9	9	9		90%
8	8	8	8	8	8	8	8	8	8	8	8		80%
7	7	7	7	7	7	7	7	7	7	7	7		70%
6	6	6	6	6	6	6	6	6	6	6	6		60%
5	5	5	5	5	5	5	5	5	5	5	5		50%
4	4	4	4	4	4	4	4	4	4	4	4		40%
3	3	3	3	3	3	3	3	3	3	3	3		30%
2	2	2	2	2	2	2	2	2	2	2	2		20%
1	1	1	1	1	1	1	1	1	1	1	1		10%

Prompt: "What time is it?" or "Show me _____."

Response: Student either says or points to the correct time.

Date:													Correct
10	10	10	10	10	10	10	10	10	10	10	10		100%
9	9	9	9	9	9	9	9	9	9	9	9		90%
8	8	8	8	8	8	8	8	8	8	8	8		80%
7	7	7	7	7	7	7	7	7	7	7	7		70%
6	6	6	6	6	6	6	6	6	6	6	6		60%
5	5	5	5	5	5	5	5	5	5	5	5		50%
4	4	4	4	4	4	4	4	4	4	4	4		40%
3	3	3	3	3	3	3	3	3	3	3	3		30%
2	2	2	2	2	2	2	2	2	2	2	2		20%
1	1	1	1	1	1	1	1	1	1	1	1		10%

Activity #7 Task Analysis: Bus Riding (Number of Prompts)

Student: _____   **Year:** _____

Task Analysis		Initials:	Initials:	Initials:	Initials:	Initials:
		Date:	Date:	Date:	Date:	Date:
		Prompts	Prompts	Prompts	Prompts	Prompts
1	Finds nearest bus stop					
2	Finds bus number					
3	Gets on correct bus					
4	Pays/shows pass					
5	Finds a seat					
6	Pulls cord prior to stop					
7	Exits the bus					
Total Number of Prompts						
Bus Stop Location						
Final Destination						

Activity #7 Task Analysis: Hand Washing (Type of Prompts)

Student: _____   **Year:** _____

Note: This data sheet is designed to track the type of prompt. Use the following key to determine which prompt was used per step. Circle the corresponding letter.

P = Physical   **G** = Gesture   **V** = Verbal   **I** = Independent

Task Analysis	Initials: Date: Prompts	Initials: Date: Prompts	Initials: Date: Prompts	Initials: Date: Prompts	Initials: Date: Prompts
1 Turns on hot/cold water	P G V I	P G V I	P G V I	P G V I	P G V I
2 Picks up soap	P G V I	P G V I	P G V I	P G V I	P G V I
3 Rubs soap on hands	P G V I	P G V I	P G V I	P G V I	P G V I
4 Rinses off soap	P G V I	P G V I	P G V I	P G V I	P G V I
5 Turns off water	P G V I	P G V I	P G V I	P G V I	P G V I
6 Dries hands	P G V I	P G V I	P G V I	P G V I	P G V I
Total Number of Physical Prompts					
Total Number of Gestural Prompts					
Total Number of Verbal Prompts					
Total Number of Independents					

Made in USA - Kendallville, IN
82986_9780996913027
09.06.2023 1318